LESS IS MORE

LESS IS MORE

Text by Claire Berrisford

An Hachette UK Company
www.hachette.co.uk

Summersdale Publishers Ltd
Part of Octopus Publishing Group Limited
Carmelite House
50 Victoria Embankment
LONDON
EC4Y 0DZ
UK

www.summersdale.com

Printed and bound in China

ISBN: 978-1-78783-577-1

Substantial discounts on bulk quantities of Summersdale books are available to corporations, professional associations and other organizations. For details contact general enquiries: telephone: +44 (0) 1243 771107 or email: enquiries@summersdale.com.

Neither the author nor the publisher can be held responsible for any loss or claim arising out of the use, or misuse, of the suggestions made herein. None of the views or suggestions in this book is intended to replace medical opinion from a doctor. If you have concerns about your health, please seek professional advice.

LESS IS MORE

FINDING JOY IN A SIMPLER LIFE

ROBIN JAMES

summersdale

CONTENTS

INTRODUCTION

If you've picked up this book, you must be searching for something.

Maybe you feel overburdened and you want to find more time in your day. Maybe you want to have more energy to do the things you love, or find a greater sense of calm. Maybe you don't know exactly what you're searching for, but you have a feeling that something is out of balance and you want to put it right.

When something is wrong, our instinct is to increase – to search out the thing that we can add to our situation to make it better. But this book proposes that we think in the opposite way: it is a guide on how to have less of what we don't need in order to make room for what we do.

By slowing down, taking a step back and embracing the idea of less, you will, in turn, find more. More time, more energy, more money, more calmness and, most importantly, more you.

If you've picked up this book, you will learn about the simple power of "less".

MORE CALM

Do you often find yourself feeling irritable and unfocused? Do you find it difficult to switch off and relax? If you find yourself answering "yes", then you might be suffering from the effects of stress.

In small amounts, stress can be healthy and motivating, but when it's a constant presence in our lives it has a negative impact on our well-being and our health. We need periods of calm and relaxation to mitigate the times when we're stressed.

Calm and stress are two ends of a spectrum so, for a happy and fulfilling life, there needs to be a balance between the two. To redress the balance, we must first look inward and reduce our levels of stress, before looking outward to proactively invite more calm into our lives.

KNOW YOURSELF

Although there are plenty of techniques you can use to calm immediate feelings of stress, the best way you can help yourself in the long term is to understand why you become stressed in the first place.

You may be able to point to big life events, such as moving house, beginning a new job or changes to your personal circumstances. However, stress can just as easily come from smaller day-to-day things. Examine your regular patterns and keep track of when you feel agitated. Perhaps it's during certain parts of your day, such as your commute, or when you're facing your to-do list. Maybe it's when you're dealing with a particular person or place. If you can't see any immediate cause, consider your lifestyle – your diet or a lack of sleep might be affecting your well-being, or perhaps you don't give yourself enough time to relax and unwind.

Of course, we are all complex individuals, so there may not be one simple answer. However, every day spent paying attention to how you are reacting to the world around you will help you to become more self-aware. Once you understand the roots of your stress and begin taking steps to deal with them, calmness should follow.

SET PEACE OF MIND AS YOUR HIGHEST GOAL AND ORGANIZE YOUR ENTIRE LIFE AROUND IT.

Brian Tracy

KNOW YOUR
body and mind

In your journey to understanding and reducing stress, it's important to learn how to listen to your body. Stress can manifest in a number of ways and most of the symptoms are easy to overlook, so it's important to know what to watch out for.

Body: Physical symptoms can include shallow breathing, headaches, dizziness, muscle tension, fatigue or changes to your appetite or libido.

Mind: You might feel overwhelmed, nervous, irritable, depressed, unable to enjoy the things you love, or like your thoughts are racing. Or you might feel restless, unable to concentrate or tearful.

In isolation, these symptoms might feel like small problems that can be explained away or ignored, but they might be part of a bigger picture about your state of mind. Being able to spot these effects as indicators of stress is a vital step on the way to being able to manage your stress and, therefore, a key process in finding balance and calm in your life.

Nothing can bring you
peace but yourself.

RALPH WALDO EMERSON

THE POWER OF BREATHING

Once you have an awareness of your stress levels and how they're influenced by the world around you, try turning your focus to reducing them.

A good place to start is with the simplest and most central part of life itself: your breath. Breathing is a reflex, so we don't often think about it. But, in fact, our breath is an incredible tool that we can harness to improve our well-being. There are a raft of benefits that conscious breathing can provide, including increased focus, better sleep and relaxation, more energy, increased positive thinking, a clearer mind and increased feelings of resilience and self-esteem. All together, these benefits combine to reduce your stress levels and instil in you a greater sense of calm.

Breathe in deeply
to bring your mind
home to your body.

Thích Nhất Hạnh

Why it works

Breathing increases the levels of oxygen in your blood, which keeps our cells and tissue healthy and helps to clear our bodies of CO_2 and other toxins in the bloodstream.

Conscious breathing can also affect the way that our bodies function. Deep, slow breaths activate the parasympathetic nervous system (PSNS) – the system that regulates our body in a resting state. Once the PSNS is triggered, it can then override the body's "fight-or-flight" stress response and help to calm you down.

BREATHING EXERCISE

Breathing is something that you can do at any point during your day to bring you stillness. Here is a simple exercise to help you slow down and deepen your breaths.

Find a quiet, uncluttered place and sit in a comfortable position. Close your eyes if you would like. Become aware of your breath, and allow your natural breathing pattern to deepen, lengthen and slow. If a thought comes into your mind, acknowledge it but don't pursue it. Remain focused on your breath. Notice if any parts of your body feel tense – if so, relax them. Let yourself be still and soft. Do this for as long as you would like to, whether that's for five minutes or for half an hour.

How to breathe

A good quality breath should be deep rather than shallow, with the air filling your abdomen rather than your chest. It should also be slow and steady, with the exhale being slightly longer than the inhale. If you can, inhale through your nose – as this warms the air and helps you to deepen your breath – and exhale through your mouth.

IF YOU WANT TO CONQUER THE ANXIETY OF LIFE, LIVE IN THE MOMENT, LIVE IN THE BREATH.

———

Amit Ray

Self-care

Self-care is anything that you do to help to protect or nurture your own health and well-being.

An act of self-care could be a mundane everyday task, or it could be an indulgent treat – it is anything that contributes to your sense of wellness and keeps you feeling happy and healthy. When we're busy and stressed, taking time out for self-care may seem like the last thing you should be doing. But it's at these times, when we feel most pressured, that we need self-care the most.

IT'S NOT
SELFISH TO
LOVE YOURSELF,
TAKE CARE OF
YOURSELF, AND
TO MAKE YOUR
HAPPINESS A
PRIORITY. IT'S
NECESSARY.

Mandy Hale

Give yourself permission

Self-care is about putting your health and your body first, but the biggest hurdle we face is often the idea of permission. When there are so many other demands on your time and energy, it may feel selfish to spend any of it on yourself... but it's not. If the idea of self-care fills you with guilt, remind yourself that you are a priority. Give yourself permission to take time out and nurture your well-being – because you cannot pour from an empty cup.

Make time for you

If you don't know where to start with self-care, think about what makes you happy and satisfied. Perhaps self-care for you could mean cooking yourself a delicious meal or listening to music. Maybe it will be phoning a friend, watching a film or going on a run. Pursuing a hobby is another effective act of self-care, as you're doing something just for the joy of it.

If you find it hard to make time for self-care, schedule it in the same way you would all your other appointments and tasks. Even if it's ten minutes to sit quietly with a cup of tea, treat it as a non-negotiable part of your plan for the day.

Self-care has become a new
priority – the revelation that it's
perfectly permissible to listen to
your body and do what it needs.

Frances Ryan

Keep up your everyday chores

Self-care doesn't just mean treating yourself to the things
that make you happy. It also means keeping up with the little
chores of day-to-day life, like brushing your teeth, doing the
laundry and washing the dishes. They may seem insignificant
or boring, but these small actions are a hugely valuable part
of looking after yourself, and keeping up with them
makes you feel calmer and more in control. If you
are feeling stressed, set yourself the task
of completing one tiny chore and see
how much better you feel once it's done.

BE YOUR OWN BEST FRIEND

If your closest friend was exhausted and overwhelmed, you wouldn't push them to keep going and do more. You also wouldn't let them say something negative and untrue about themselves, or let them think that they weren't worth spending time on. So why would you say these things to yourself? Self-care is about treating yourself the same way you would treat your best friend. Honour your needs and be kind to yourself.

SELF-COMPASSION IS SIMPLY GIVING THE SAME KINDNESS TO OURSELVES THAT WE WOULD GIVE TO OTHERS.

Christopher Germer

TINY MOMENTS
of self-care

Have breakfast
in bed.

Cloud-watch.

Take a
hot shower.

Spend five minutes doodling,
colouring or drawing.

Stroke
your pet.

Open the
windows
and listen
to the birds.

Watch a sunrise
or sunset.

Have a
cuddle.

Watch the shadows
on the ground.

Give yourself a
hand massage.

Write a postcard.

Walk
barefoot.

Light a candle.

Savour a hot drink on
a chilly day, or a cold
one on a hot day.

Read a chapter
of a book.

Meditate.

Listen to your
favourite song.

Smile; think
about something
that makes
you happy.

Go for a
five-minute stroll.

STRETCH OUT

Regular stretching can work wonders for our bodies and minds. Not only does it help to reduce fatigue, improve posture and circulation, but, as one of the many physical symptoms of stress is tension in our muscles, it also promotes a feeling of calm. Stretching even just for 30 seconds at a time is a way to release the tension and feel more composed.

Shoulder stretch

Raise your arms above your head, lock your fingers together and turn your palms so they're facing upward. Try to stretch your hands up while keeping your shoulders down. Hold this for a few breaths before bringing your hands down again.

Chest stretch

Stand up with your feet hip-width apart and look straight ahead. Clasp your hands behind you and then lift them as high as you can. This stretch is particularly good if you spend a lot of time at a computer or desk as it counteracts the effects of hunching over a screen.

Health is a state of
complete harmony of the
body, mind and spirit.

B. K. S. Iyengar

Hamstring stretch

Stand with your feet hip-width apart. Bend
forward from the hips as far as you can go,
keeping your neck and shoulders relaxed. Wrap
your hands around the backs of your legs and
hold the stretch for 30 seconds. Bend your
knees, hold your stomach in and roll up slowly.

Hip stretch

Kneel up on the floor. Keep one knee on the
floor, and bring the other leg up in front
of you so it creates a right angle with your
body. Keeping your hips square, gently
lunge forward until you feel a stretch down
the front of your back leg. Hold for a few
seconds and repeat on the other leg.

MORE SLEEP

Our day begins the moment we open our eyes and ends when we close them. Or does it? Sleep can seem to be an inevitable part of our routines, or even wasted time, but it shouldn't be dismissed, because it's just as important as diet and exercise in keeping us healthy and balanced.

Sleep is an extraordinary process, whereby your body heals itself, regulates hormones, processes information and consolidates memories. Good sleep also improves your immune system, focus, energy levels and mood – and most of us don't get enough of it. Although there are many reasons for this, distractions, either internal or external, are a common culprit.

Read the tips in this chapter to find out how to minimize the distractions that disrupt our sleep and soothe yourself – because the better your sleep, the better your waking life will be.

HAVE A ROUTINE

As well as bringing focus to the end of your day and eliminating distractions, a bedtime routine is a simple way to programme your body and mind, helping you to prepare for sleep.

The most important part of your routine is timing: aim to go to bed at the same time each night, as this will help your body clock to get into a steady rhythm.

Your routine could also include little rituals to help you wind down. Perhaps you could have a bath, followed by a hot drink. You could read a chapter of a book, fill in a journal, meditate or do some relaxing yoga. Whatever you choose, the important thing is consistency. If you keep to your routine, eventually, these regular pre-bedtime activities will help to signal to your body and mind that it's time to switch off and go to sleep.

The best bridge between despair and hope is a good night's sleep.

E. JOSEPH COSSMAN

MAKE YOUR ROOM A SANCTUARY

Your bedroom should be a place that you enjoy spending time in, and that helps you to feel relaxed, so make sure that it's enticing. Keep your bedding clean and fresh, and air out the room every day if you can. It's also important to keep it tidy, as it's difficult to truly relax in a room that's cluttered. Make sure that the things in your bedroom are either the essentials, or only trinkets and items that you love. This is especially important if your bedroom is a small space, as keeping it clean and clutter free will give the illusion of a more spacious room.

Making your bedroom a sanctuary also means leaving your to-do list and everyday responsibilities in another room. Keep your laundry basket outside your bedroom, for instance, and avoid doing work in bed. Your bedroom should be for sleep and sex only – a place that you associate with rest and relaxation.

BE SCREEN-FREE

Our circadian rhythm is our bodies' natural sleep/wake cycle. This cycle is regulated by a delicate balance of hormones which are influenced by our exposure to light: as it gets dark we begin to wind down and become sleepier, and when the sun rises and the light increases, we start to wake up.

Screens tend to disrupt this cycle, because they emit blue light. This kind of light has the same effect on your brain as bright daylight, so it interrupts your body's natural rhythm and prevents you from becoming sleepy. So, for a good night's sleep, we should avoid looking at screens for at least 30 minutes, if not an hour, before going to bed.

To help with this resolution, try leaving your phone in a different room, as this is also an easy way to avoid distractions at bedtime. Whether you can't resist the sound of a notification, or you are forever looking things up or replying to emails, separation from your phone is a way to make a strong distinction between the daytime – when you are engaged and alert – and night-time – when you are calm and restful.

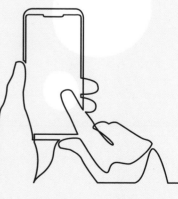

TIPS FOR BETTER SLEEP

When you have a calm and focused bedtime environment, here are a few tips to help you drop off:

A hot bath: Your body cools down as you fall asleep; having a hot bath warms you up – which then triggers your body into cooling you down, and easing you into sleep.

Pillow shape: Ensure that your pillow is the right shape, height and softness for your body and sleeping position. There are many different options to explore, and finding the perfect match can improve your sleep.

Temperature: The optimum room temperature to promote good sleep is between 16 and 18°C (60–64°F).

Earplugs: If you are a light sleeper, use earplugs to muffle the noise around you.

Consistency: Try to get up at roughly the same time each day – even at the weekend – as this helps to maintain your sleep pattern.

Darkness: A dark room helps to signal to your brain that it's time to sleep, so turn off any lights or electrical items and use heavy curtains. Alternatively, try using an eye mask.

BREATHE YOURSELF TO SLEEP

The 4–7–8 breathing technique is a simple but effective exercise to help still your mind and soothe you to sleep.

1. Find a place where you can sit or lie comfortably.

2. Place the tip of your tongue against the tissue just above your front teeth. Keep it there throughout the exercise.

3. Empty your lungs completely.

4. Breathe in quietly through your nose for four seconds.

5. Hold the breath for seven seconds.

6. Exhale through your mouth for eight seconds, allowing the breath to make a slight "whoosh" sound through your lips as you do so.

7. Repeat this cycle another three times.

If you can't hold your breath for the full seven seconds, try shorter intervals at first: breathe in for two seconds, hold for three seconds, and breathe out for four.

If you would like further support, you can download apps which guide you through the technique.

Golden milk

Curling up with a hot drink before bedtime is not only comforting, but it helps us to pause, unwind and have a moment of stillness to round off the day. Try adding this recipe into your bedtime routine. The nostalgic comfort of warm milk combines with the antioxidative properties of turmeric, which can help to protect against sleep deprivation.

Ingredients

240 ml (1 cup) milk (any variety)

1 tsp ground turmeric

½ tsp ground cinnamon

½ tsp ground ginger

½ tsp honey or maple syrup (optional)

Makes: 1 cup

Method

Place the milk, turmeric, cinnamon and ginger in a small saucepan and heat gently, stirring constantly.

When the milk is hot (steaming but not boiling), remove from the heat and test the flavour with a teaspoon.

Stir in honey or maple syrup if desired, and add more spice if you prefer a stronger flavour.

Transfer the milk to your favourite mug, make yourself cosy and enjoy.

Extra: Add in a tiny pinch of ground cloves and star anise for extra depth of flavour.

Bedtime MILK DRINKS

There are many ways you can enjoy a cup of warm milk before bedtime. Here are a few ideas. Simply add these ingredients to any variety of hot milk:

Stir in 1 tsp honey

One caffeine-free masala chai teabag

1 tbsp cocoa, ½ tsp sweetener and a pinch of chilli powder

1 drop vanilla essence and ½ tsp sweetener

½ tsp cinnamon, ½ tsp ginger, pinch nutmeg and 1 tsp sweetener

Natural sweeteners

Honey, agave nectar, real maple syrup, stevia or coconut sugar.

If you want a soothing hot drink without milk, choose non-caffeinated herbal teas. Those that feature lavender, camomile, vanilla, hops or valerian can also help to promote a restful night's sleep.

WRITE IT OUT

A distraction many of us face when trying to sleep is mental chatter. When we quieten down and are no longer preoccupied by the physical tasks of the day, our thoughts often seem to get louder.

If you find yourself with racing thoughts, or a mind that won't let you rest, try putting pen to paper. Write a to-do list, so that all the jobs you keep remembering are not forgotten, or write a journal entry to channel and express your feelings. Writing is therapeutic, and the action can help to put a little distance between you and your thoughts, giving you space to find calm and drift off to sleep.

IF YOU CAN'T SLEEP...

Try not to worry about the fact that you're not asleep, as this will make the task harder. Get out of bed and do something else that you find relaxing: read a book, do some yoga, make a hot drink or go for a walk. When you feel sleepy, try going back to bed. If the problem is prolonged, seek advice from a medical professional.

IF YOU DIDN'T GET ENOUGH SLEEP...

If you haven't had a good night's sleep, there are ways to boost your energy throughout the day. Stay hydrated by drinking plenty of water, take breaks throughout the day to get sunlight and fresh air, and snack on fruit or foods rich in protein, such as nuts or yoghurt. If you can, try taking a 20-minute power nap to keep you feeling refreshed and alert.

MORE TIME

Have you ever wished that there were more hours in a day? Do you feel like you're being pushed from one task to the next, barely able to take a breath? Does it feel like time slips away before you have time to do the things you want to do?

Three characteristics of modern life are that it is busy, fast and full. We face pressures from society, our workplace, and our friends and families to do more, to take on more responsibilities and to give away more of our time – and this puts us out of balance.

The key to redressing the balance is putting quality over quantity. We cannot create more time – and we don't need to. Instead, we can be wiser about how we spend the time that we have. This usually means doing less and making sure that the things that we choose to do are done with intention.

Say "YES" to saying "NO"

We're conditioned to say "yes" to the things people ask of us – helping out with an extra task at work that we don't have time for, meeting up with someone because we feel we should, or lending a hand in fundraisers or family events out of a sense of duty. The simple truth is: we can't satisfy everybody – so we should stop trying to. When we say "yes" to everything, we spread ourselves too thin. We end up filling our time until there's no space left to breathe, and this invites resentment, stress and exhaustion.

To begin doing less, the first step is to see "no" as a positive and freeing word. Next time you are asked to do an extra job, whether it's at work or at home, assess your schedule and decide whether you want to take it on, whether you have time to, and what effect it might have on your well-being. If you need to say "no", then don't be afraid to do so. Remember that declining can often be the healthiest choice, because you need to have the energy to look after yourself before you can help others.

> You can be a good person with a kind heart and still say no.
>
> LORI DESCHENE

GET COMFORTABLE WITH "NO"

Saying "no" can be incredibly challenging, especially if we have to say it to people we respect and care about. However, for a truly balanced life, we need to be able to do it, and to be comfortable with the fact that "no" is a full sentence.

To help yourself to feel happier with "no", put pen to paper. Write down all the times you've said "yes" in the past week. Think about which ones you actually wanted to say "yes" to, which ones you're already regretting, and which ones you should have declined. It'll soon become clear why an unconsidered "yes" can be more damaging to us than an honest "no".

DO IT WITH PURPOSE

Although taking on tasks for other people is one drain on our time, our own lack of focus is often just as much to blame. How often have you had a stretch of time before you – maybe a Sunday afternoon, or a free evening after work – and somehow had it slip away before you've had a chance to do something worthwhile?

Take control of your free time, whether it's half an hour or a whole day. Rather than whiling the time away, decide what you're going to do before you do it – even if you decide that you're going to do absolutely nothing! Defining what you do before you do it gives your actions purpose, and allows you to claim that time as your own.

KEEP TRACK OF TIME

Creating more time for yourself is about using it well. Consider budgeting your time in the same way that you'd budget your money.

To do this, you need a picture of where your time goes, so try keeping a diary of your time for a few days or a week, including as much detail as possible. When you have enough data, ask yourself: what are your habits and patterns, and are you happy with them? If you have goals you want to reach or hobbies you want to pursue, does your current lifestyle allow time for these things?

All we have to decide
is what to do with the
time that is given us.

J. R. R. Tolkien

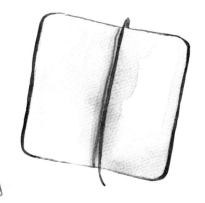

You will probably discover that there are little pockets of your day that drain time more than others. Perhaps you watch TV out of habit, or you take a long time planning your food in the evenings. Perhaps you have a habit of procrastinating, or you take a long time to switch from one task to the next.

Once you're aware of your daily patterns, you can make small changes to help yourself to use the time more effectively, such as only watching TV that you want to watch, planning your meals in advance, or writing a to-do list to help you manage multiple tasks.

MASTER YOUR TO-DO LIST

When managed properly, a to-do list can give you peace of mind and boost your productivity. Here's how to master the art of the to-do list, and how to stop it from becoming an overwhelming and unmanageable ream of tasks.

1 Write a master list

Write a list of everything that needs doing – even the tiny things should be included.

2 Break it down

Look at the big tasks and break them down into smaller steps that you can take to complete them.

3 Prioritize

Go through your list and rank each job by its importance. For instance, write a "1" next to the most urgent and a "3" for the least urgent, or colour-code each item.

4 Take it one day at a time

Instead of working directly from the master list, begin a new list for each day and pick a small number of things that you will be able to accomplish.

✓ _____

✓ _____

Top tips

Try the 1–3–5 method. This means picking one big task for the day, three medium-sized ones and five small things. You don't have to use these exact numbers, but this tiered structure keeps your to-do list realistic and manageable, as it prevents you from trying to tackle too much in one day.

Make sure everything on your list is a specific task. For instance, instead of "Plan holiday", you could decide to "Book flights" or "Find accommodation".

Record your progress. Include tick boxes so you can see items being crossed off the list, or keep an "I did" list as well as your master to-do list.

Apps such as Trello and Wunderlist can help you organize your to-do list digitally if you don't want to keep track of paper.

✓ _____

✓ _____

THE *KANBAN* METHOD

Kanban is a Japanese system originally developed for use in manufacturing – but it translates well to the personal to-do list as well. This method allows you to visualize your work, and the unique benefit is that it limits the number of tasks you can work on at any one time. If you have a tendency to overestimate how much you can tackle at once, this might be a good technique to try.

To try it for yourself, draw three columns labelled "To do", "In progress" and "Done". Then follow these steps:

You will need:
- A sheet of paper or a whiteboard
- Sticky notes

To do	In progress	Done
Write each task on a sticky note and place in this column. Organize them by priority if you can, or by colour if you'd like.	Choose a task to do and move it to this column. This is what you will focus on today. You should have no more than three tasks in this column at once.	Move sticky notes to this column when they are complete.

ONE CANNOT
MANAGE TOO
MANY AFFAIRS:
LIKE PUMPKINS
IN THE WATER,
ONE POPS UP
WHILE YOU TRY
TO HOLD DOWN
THE OTHER.

Chinese proverb

THE *Pomodoro* TECHNIQUE

This technique is an effective way to focus yourself on your tasks. It's the to-do list equivalent of a sprint compared to a marathon, as it involves working in short, sharp bursts.

1. Look at your to-do list for the day and break it into 25-minute chunks.

2. Set a timer for 25 minutes and work solidly for that time.

3. Have a 5-minute break.

4. Repeat steps two and three thrice more.

5. Have a break for 15–30 minutes.

6. Repeat this process until the end of your working day.

Take care of the
minutes and the
hours will take care
of themselves.

LORD CHESTERFIELD

MORE ENERGY

When we have enough energy, we come alive. These are the days when we feel our best, and often our happiest – when we can take everything in our stride, tackle the tasks of the day, and reach for new heights.

So how can we have more of these days? Our energy levels are linked to our health, so looking after our bodies is one of the best ways to promote a feeling of vitality and wellness.

For many of us, it's challenging to maintain a healthy lifestyle, and thinking about it in terms of "more" – how to eat *more* healthy food, how to do *more* exercise – only increases stress, as we have to think about how we will cram yet more things into our already busy days. Instead, this chapter proposes that we approach wellness more mindfully, aiming to minimize the unhealthier elements of our daily lives, and basing our choices around what will nourish our minds and bodies.

Eat well to feel well

A healthy diet includes:

- Five portions of fruit and vegetables a day.

- Plenty of water – aim for six to eight cups a day (approx. 2 litres (3 ½ pints)).

- Healthy fats, such as those in nuts, seeds and oily fish.

- Protein, which can be found in beans, pulses, eggs, fish and chicken.

- Meals based around carbohydrates such as bread, rice and pasta.

- Iron-rich foods, such as red meat, green leafy vegetables or fortified cereals.

Top tips for energy

Eating three meals a day at regularly spaced intervals will maintain your blood sugar levels. Not only does this regulate hunger levels, but it keeps you feeling alert and awake.

Vitamins B and C are particularly good for promoting healthy brain function, and can be found in citrus fruits and leafy vegetables.

Starchy carbohydrates – such as potatoes, bread, cereals, pasta and rice – should make up approximately a third of your diet. They are full of nutrients and one of the body's main sources of energy.

Less is more

You don't have to overhaul your whole lifestyle – making small, healthy choices every day goes a long way to making you feel healthier and happier. Consider swapping out salty or sugary snacks for something healthier, and enjoy processed foods in moderation. Try to minimize your alcohol consumption, or opt for non-alcoholic alternatives, as alcohol is a depressant and can disturb your sleep, impacting your energy levels.

BREAKFAST IDEAS

A nourishing breakfast gets you ready to tackle the challenges of the day. Here are some ideas:

Cereal

Granola

Boiled egg

Poached egg and spinach on toast

Avocado and pumpkin seeds on toast

Porridge

Pancakes with fruit

LUNCH IDEAS

Fuel up and bring some colour to
your lunchtimes with these ideas:

Wrap filled with
fresh salad

Salad jars

Salad-filled sandwich in a wholemeal roll

Grilled chicken and vegetable lunch box

Quinoa salad

DINNER IDEAS

These dinner ideas are delicious, satisfying and, best of all, full of healthy fats and nutrients to keep you feeling full:

Chickpea curry
with naan

Pasta with pesto
sauce and vegetables

Grilled chicken with
quinoa and vegetables

Baked tomatoes and egg with pitta bread

Stir-fry with chicken
and peppers

Grilled salmon and
steamed vegetables

SNACK IDEAS

Try any of these snacks to give
you a healthy boost through the day:

Granola bars

Blueberries

Nuts

Yoghurt

Energy balls

Carrot sticks and hummus

GET MOVING

Exercise has a raft of benefits for our minds and bodies. It can reduce stress and anxiety and increase confidence and self-esteem; it increases the production of endorphins, which create positive feelings and ease pain; and it enhances brain sensitivity to serotonin, which relieves feelings of depression. This all adds up to a boost in our energy levels.

You don't have to spend hours in the gym every week. As long as you're moving and you have increased your heart rate, you will feel the benefits of exercise. This means that even small amounts of physical activity can still reap huge rewards, and there are plenty of ways to fit it into your day. In an ideal world, we should be raising our heart rate three times a week to stay healthy – this is a good goal to work toward.

Get off the bus one stop early and walk the rest of the way.

Walk a slightly longer route than normal to get to your destination, whether it's to work, to the shop, or to the letter box.

If you're waiting for the kettle to boil, use the time to do jumping jacks, wall push-ups or squats, or lift kettlebells (or something else that's heavy, such as a bag of sugar or a litre bottle of water).

Take the stairs rather than the lift.

If you sit down for long periods at work, try to get up every half an hour and have a short burst of activity: walk up and down the stairs, do ten lunges, or even do a quick yoga stretch.

Cleaning is a workout too – put extra energy into hoovering or scrubbing.

Do a strength and conditioning session while you watch your favourite programme instead of sitting on the sofa, or do some jumping jacks as a cardio exercise.

Try run commuting, which is running all or part of the way home from work.

Sit on a stability ball rather than a chair.

Go for a walk or have a game of Frisbee or rounders with your friends instead of sitting in a coffee shop or pub.

Take the dog for a run rather than a walk.

Put on some music and dance! Dance while you clean, tidy or do other odd jobs around the house, or dance just because.

GET EXERCISING

If you want to devote more time to being active, try swapping out some of your downtime for longer exercise sessions. Exercising is a wonderful act of self-care, and if you want to block out more time in your day to look out for your well-being, these activities are a great place to start.

Running

Running is simple and free, and it's easily adaptable to your location and fitness levels. You need very little to get started – just throw on comfy clothes, tie your trainers and go. Sign up for a race if you want a goal to work toward, or try parkrun if you want to run with others in a friendly, supportive community. If you're a beginner, you could download the Couch to 5K app, which will help to build up your ability safely and healthily.

Swimming

Swimming is a great full-body workout. It's a form of resistance training as you have to move your whole body against the water, and it keeps your heart rate up too. It's also a great option if you don't want to put too much strain on your joints.

Being active every day
makes it easier to hear
that inner voice.

Haruki Murakami

Join a team or a class

Try team sports, such as football, rugby, lacrosse or volleyball, or join a dance, Zumba or Pilates class. Not only are these activities all a good cardio workout, but in a team or class environment you will make new connections and develop skills that can benefit you in other parts of life too, such as resilience, teamwork and discipline.

Climbing or bouldering

This is a good activity to try with a friend and it will improve your strength and endurance – plus it often doesn't feel like exercise. It's also a great way to push your own boundaries and challenge yourself to conquer your fears and do more than you think you can.

MORE MONEY

Whether we like it or not, money plays a huge role in our lives, and it often has a significant hand in determining our general mood and outlook. When things are going well, money gives us a sense of safety and security, but when we have concerns about debt or overspending, it is a major cause of stress.

To have more money, we don't necessarily need to earn more. As well as tips on getting the most out of what we have, this chapter focuses on how to find more money by spending less, and by spending better.

TOP MONEY-SAVING TIPS

Make use of charity shops, car boot sales, eBay, Facebook Marketplace and other online initiatives when you're browsing for gifts, clothes or household items.

Cancel subscriptions you don't need.

Repair clothes rather than throwing them away.

Invite friends over to your house rather than going out.

Do your research: make sure you're getting the cheapest deals for your gas, electricity, heating, phone bills and insurance.

Buy supermarket brands rather than the specialist brands.

If you're booking hotels or plane tickets online, do your research in a private browser window so that your data isn't collected. This prevents sites from hiking up prices the next time you visit.

To save on train travel, look at whether you can split your ticket. Buying your journey in two halves is sometimes cheaper than buying a ticket for the whole journey.

Look for sites online where you can swap your items, such as Depop.

Use Freecycle, a site where you can offer to rehome other people's unwanted items for free. You can also put out a request for items that you are looking for.

Start a loose change jar – the pennies add up.

Make coffee at home and bring it with you in a flask or insulated cup.

Cook at home more than you eat out.

Protect yourself against small impulse purchases, as these accumulate. Next time you want to buy something, make yourself wait. If you still want it after a couple of hours, then consider buying it.

Write a list before you go food shopping to avoid buying what you don't need.

If you smoke, cut down or give up the habit.

Set your heating so that it's only on when you're in the house.

Cook meals in large batches and freeze your extra portions, because buying ingredients in bulk is cheaper.

Look for discount codes and vouchers: get a meal out for half price or money off your weekly shop.

Buy seasonal cards and gifts in the sales. For instance, buy next year's Christmas cards at the end of December and save them for the following year.

Consider making gifts by hand; making candles, soap, baked goods, painting or drawing, or knitting a scarf are just some options. Alternatively, give the gift of time. Offer to do gardening, cleaning or babysitting for your friends and family.

TRY *KAKEIBO*

To truly combat money worries we need to be in control of our finances, which means knowing exactly where our money is going. For this, the *kakeibo* method is a great place to start.

This method helps you to keep track of what you spend, a month at a time, by asking you to categorize each transaction. By the end of the month, you will have a comprehensive picture of your outgoings and a way to prioritize what really matters to you.

You will need an A4 piece of paper per month of expenditure. Alternatively, invest in a notebook specifically for bookkeeping. That way, all your records will be in one place.

The method is made up of four questions:

How much money do you have?

Take an A4 piece of paper or a page of your notebook. At the top, write down your monthly income, minus all the fixed costs, such as rent and monthly bills.

How much are you spending?

Divide your paper up into four columns, one with each of the following headings:

- **Survival:** Regular, necessary expenditure, such as food, childcare and transport costs.

- **Culture:** Expenditure on cultural activities, theatre, books, the cinema, museums or magazines.

- **Optional:** Anything you choose to spend money on, like having dinner out, social events, shopping or takeaways.

- **Extra:** Anything irregular or unexpected, such as birthday presents or repairs around the house.

Over the next month, record everything you spend in the relevant column, no matter how small. Try to be as realistic as you can; for instance, it may feel like you *needed* that new top or that cup of coffee, but it's more likely that these would count as "optional" spends rather than "survival".

At the end of the month, take stock of your outgoings. How does it compare to your monthly income? Are you spending significantly more in one area than another?

Total income per month: **£1200**
Income minus fixed costs: **£540**

MONTH: JUNE

Survival		Culture		Optional		Extra	
Food shop	**£42.35**	Cinema	**£11.95**	Dinner out	**£23.27**	B-day card	**£2.50**
Bus fare	**£3.50**			Work drinks	**£18.50**		
Food shop	**£13.20**			New dress	**£19.99**		

How much money do you want to save?

Do you want to go on a holiday? Are you saving up for a car, a house or a gift? Or would you simply like to have some spare money left over at the end of the month? Think about where you would like to be and set yourself achievable goals.

Remember to think about how you will achieve these goals too. Look at where you spend the most and try to identify areas where you can cut costs. Perhaps you can pack your own lunch instead of buying it out, opt for basic food brands rather than premium ones or visit charity shops to find second-hand books, clothes and films to enjoy rather than always buying brand new.

How can you improve?

This is more of a question to start asking yourself once you have three or four months' data to hand. Have you achieved your savings goals? If not, investigate why this is. Is the goal unrealistic, or is there an area where you're still overspending? Make a new goal for the following month, making a change either to your savings goal or to your spending habits. On the other hand, if you have reached your goal, are you happy with this or do you want to save more?

IF YOU WOULD
BE WEALTHY,
THINK OF
SAVING AS
WELL AS
GETTING.

—

Benjamin Franklin

NO-SPEND DAYS

Being conscious about what you spend doesn't mean that you can't have fun. There are a whole host of things you can enjoy that don't put pressure on your bank balance.

Have a scavenger hunt; choose a theme and then go looking! You could find a collection of green items, things beginning with the letter S, or things that you find beautiful.

Visit a local museum or art gallery, as many of them have free entry.

Host a games night.

Go to the park – bring a picnic and make an afternoon of it.

Listen to a podcast and learn something new.

Have a day of outdoor games with your friends. Think rounders, volleyball, Frisbee, or even the childhood classic: tag.

Look up what's on in your local community – from craft fairs to music events, there's usually something free to experience.

Watch the sunrise or sunset.

Go to the beach.

See the sights of your city. Explore as if you're a tourist!

Go for a run – use it as a way to explore somewhere new in your local area.

Watch a DVD or read a book that's been sitting on your shelf for ages.

Go to a farmers' market and sample the food.

Have a romantic evening in – just you, your partner and quality time.

Do a jigsaw.

Volunteer your time for a good cause.

Get creative – draw, paint, sing, write or dance. Whatever medium takes your fancy, use today to try it out.

Settle down on your own or with friends and have a movie marathon.

MORE SPACE

Decluttering is a way of putting quality above quantity, which is the message at the heart of this book. It's the idea that more does not always mean more, and that a single thing that is savoured, cherished or well chosen brings far more joy to your life than three things that aren't.

This thoughtful approach to life can be liberating, as it means that you are able to let go of the things that you don't need to make more room for the things that matter.

You can apply this thinking to most areas of life, but it's particularly meaningful when applied to the home. This chapter contains all the tips you need to reduce life's clutter and help you to focus on the things that you love – which will give you the space you need, mentally and physically, to breathe and be yourself.

DECLUTTERING

Decluttering is the mindful approach to tidying your home. Despite the images it brings to mind, it's not about throwing everything away, or trying to whittle your belongings down to the bare minimum. It simply means taking stock of the things that you have, and letting go of anything that is unnecessary. It's a way of making sure that the things you have are the things you use and love – and that you have exactly what you need, no more and no less.

It's a simple activity, but its effects are wide-reaching. Your home is a sanctuary, and having a tidy and organized space to come back to can have a hugely positive effect on your mood and your outlook on life. It's also easier to relax in a space that's tidy.

The very act of tidying can be therapeutic too; making small but confident decisions about what you do and don't need allows you to check in with yourself and your life, and helps you to feel in control.

HOW TO *declutter*

For many of us, decluttering can be challenging to
begin with: not only can it be tedious, but it forces us to
confront ourselves and make tough decisions. If the idea of
decluttering is daunting, think about it in a positive light.
Depending on where you are in your life it could be a form
of therapy or catharsis, or it could represent a fresh start.

To begin, pick one area of your home. It could be your
wardrobe, a particular room, or even just one drawer.
Go through everything you find in that area item by
item, and sort each one into the following piles: things
to keep, things to throw away and things to rehome.

When you're sorting through your possessions, the
most important thing is that you're realistic and honest
with yourself. The phrase "just in case" is a red flag;
if you find yourself using it, think hard about whether
you really need to keep the item you're considering.

The ability to be objective, and to let things go when you
honestly don't need them is a great skill to learn, as it can
help you to prioritize in other areas of your life too.

A HOME FOR EVERYTHING

Decluttering isn't just about reducing the amount that you own. It's also about being smart with how you store your possessions and making your space work for you. Here are a few ideas about how you can be inventive with storage:

- Put a hanging shoe rack on the back of a door to store all kinds of items – from jewellery to toys.
- Put small storage boxes on your shelves instead of just stacking your belongings in a pile – this makes the space far more versatile.
- Hang your ironing board on hooks on the back of a door.
- For organized clothes storage, roll your clothes in drawers rather than folding them.
- Use tension rods to hang under-the-sink cleaning products or to turn an alcove into extra wardrobe space.

Use wasted space

Our homes tend to have a lot of "wasted" space, such as the area under the sofa, under the bed, or on top of the fridge or wardrobe. These are great places to store seasonal clothes, or things that you only use occasionally, such as craft supplies, sleeping bags or wrapping paper. Simply find a box the right size for your space, put your belongings in and slot the box into place – and you have a tidier, more organized home.

HAVE NOTHING IN YOUR HOUSES THAT YOU DO NOT KNOW TO BE USEFUL OR BELIEVE TO BE BEAUTIFUL.

William Morris

TINY, TIDY MOMENTS

Although decluttering is a great way to tidy your home, no matter how thoroughly you do it there will always be little things that you can't get rid of but that are also hard to keep presentable. Here are a few simple storage tricks:

Kitchen

Use a jam jar or cookie jar to store the necessary bits and bobs that would otherwise hang around the kitchen and dining area, such as pens, Post-its, elastic bands or pegs.

Bathroom

Hook a waterproof hanging basket in the shower to keep your soaps and shampoos organized and out of the way.

> Clutter is not just the stuff on your floor – it's anything that stands between you and the life you want to be living.

Peter Walsh

Bedroom

Repurpose an ice-cube tray and use the wells to keep your jewellery organized and easy to access.

Desk

Organize your desk drawers by making dividers out of cereal boxes. Simply draw a line around the bottom of the box the same depth as your drawer, then cut. You should be left with a small rectangular tray. Make as many as will fit in your drawer. You can then use them to organize your stationery and other desk items.

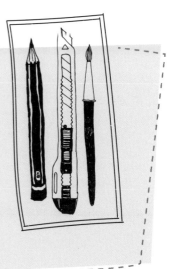

Clutter-free GIFTS

Gift giving is another part of life that tends to result in unnecessary clutter. If you have a friend or family member who is hard to buy for, consider gifting them a token that they will enjoy: a book token for the bookworm, a craft shop token for the creative friend, or an iTunes voucher for the music lover, for example. Another idea is to buy an experience – tickets to the cinema, a voucher for their favourite restaurant or a spa treatment. There are plenty of online shops that cater for these kinds of presents, and there are hundreds of options to choose from.

You could give a donation on your friend's behalf: give money to a charity that has meaning to the recipient, plant a tree in their name or sponsor an animal. Again, there are many online retailers that offer this kind of gift; try www.goodgifts.org, or www.oxfamunwrapped.com for ideas.

Why not gift your time by offering to do the gardening, cleaning or babysitting for a friend? It might seem like a small gesture, but to the recipient it will speak volumes, as it shows that you truly care.

You could also get creative. Put together a games-night package, plan a movie marathon with your friend's favourite films, or create a handmade voucher promising afternoon tea, a homecooked meal or a picnic together.

Things don't
matter, people do.

ROSIE THOMAS

FRIENDSHIP DETOX

Quality over quantity isn't only a mantra to be used when thinking about our home environment. We can also use it when thinking about the people we choose to spend our time with.

Our friendships are a defining aspect of our lives. As the saying goes, friends are the family we choose for ourselves, so if you find yourself with friends who make you feel bad about yourself and bring you down, friends who drain your time and energy, or friends who you dread meeting up with – then they probably aren't such good friends. Our friends should boost us, encourage us and make us feel valued, and if yours don't, then it may be time to take stock.

Bear in mind that friendships naturally ebb and flow. Sometimes you will disagree or misunderstand each other, so if you have an issue then talk it out. To clear the air, perhaps they need to apologize – or perhaps *you* do.

If the relationship is still bringing you down, don't be afraid to distance yourself from them for a time, and see how you feel. It can be a daunting step to take, but for a happy and balanced life, we need to be surrounded by people who care about us. A few close friends who love and support you are far more worthwhile than a larger number of friends who only know you a little.

A GOOD FRIEND
IS A CONNECTION
TO LIFE – A TIE TO
THE PAST, A ROAD
TO THE FUTURE,
THE KEY TO SANITY
IN A TOTALLY
INSANE WORLD.

Lois Wyse

MORE
SUSTAINABILITY

Of all the instances where we can say less is more, perhaps none is more significant than when we are talking about our planet. We're all familiar with the plight of the world: our seas are full of chemicals, the landscape is strewn with plastic and the earth is overflowing with waste. Our global problem is that too much is produced in order to be thrown away, so to have a bright future, we need to use less, to burn less and to waste less.

If we are going to make a difference, the whole world needs to act – but in the face of such a challenge, it's easy to feel overwhelmed and powerless. So, we must remember: change doesn't only happen on a large scale. It also comes in increments, with hundreds of tiny actions adding up to make a real difference.

This chapter covers the many small choices we can make every day that can help to reduce the amount that we waste. In turn, not only do we save money and time, and contribute to our own well-being, but, together, we are working toward saving the well-being of the planet.

Reuse and recycle

There are many easy ways that we can reuse and recycle in our day-to-day lives:

- Save citrus-fruit peel to add to your bath. The hot water brings out the essential oils, so you can enjoy a spa experience for free.

- Some items that we tend to think of as single-use can be used multiple times: kitchen foil can be unfolded and reused, sandwich bags can be washed and margarine tubs can be used as containers for the freezer.

- Old T-shirts can be used as cleaning rags and dusters, or as an alternative to bubble wrap if you are posting or moving breakable items. If you like being creative, they can be braided together to make rugs or bath mats – tutorials for these can be found online.

- A mesh fruit/vegetable bag can be scrunched up and used as a scrubber in the kitchen.

- Egg shells can be scattered on your garden as a natural, waste-free slug and snail repellent. Coffee grounds can also be distributed to help nourish your soil.

- A used teabag can be turned into a bin freshener: wait until it's dry, add a few drops of essential oil and place at the bottom of the bin.

- Used teabags can also be used to shine mirrors. Take a wet (but not dripping) teabag and wipe your mirror. Then buff it with a soft cloth, using circular motions to make the glass shine.

- Jam jars can be used to store dry goods – such as rice, sugar, flour or salt – in the cupboard and leftover food or sauce in the fridge, or they can be turned into pen pots, small planters or handy containers for string or twine.

- Old toothbrushes can be demoted to household cleaning duty and be used to clean delicate or intricate items.

THE EARTH IS A FINE PLACE AND WORTH THE FIGHTING FOR.

Ernest Hemingway

FUROSHIKI

Millions of tonnes of wrapping paper end up in landfill sites every year. Designed for only a single use and often coated with a layer of plastic, it's a serious culprit in the contamination of Planet Earth. Using brown paper or newspaper is a good step toward making your gift giving more eco-friendly, as it can be recycled. But why not go one step further and try *furoshiki*?

Furoshiki is a traditional kind of Japanese cloth. It's used to wrap all manner of objects – from clothes to lunch boxes – but it makes a particularly attractive way to present gifts. *Furoshiki* are square shaped and often sport beautiful prints and patterns, and the finished products swathed in these cloths appear elegant and classy. Best of all, it's reusable, so nothing is wasted.

Here are some simple ways to wrap objects in cloth:

How to wrap a bottle

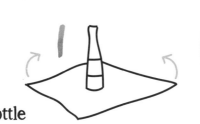

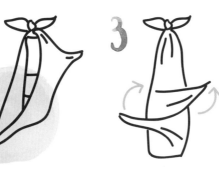

How to wrap a book or small box

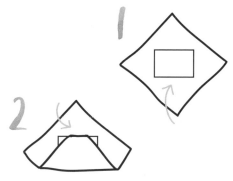

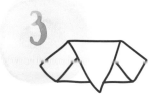

REDUCE FOOD WASTE

The world throws away millions of tonnes of food every year – needlessly. Not only is this a waste of our money, as we buy food that we then don't eat, but farming and producing food requires vast amounts of energy, so by throwing it away we are wasting our resources and putting unnecessary strain on the environment. However, we can effect change, and it starts with us, in our own kitchens. Here are a few easy tips to help us to reduce food waste in our homes:

Buy products that will remain in date for when you plan to cook them. Try not to be taken in by offers where you end up buying more food than necessary.

Make the most of leftovers. For example, use a roast chicken carcass or vegetable peelings to make stock for soups and casseroles.

Freeze meat, fish, eggs, milk, cheese, bread, fruit and vegetables to extend the life of your food. Check online to see how long certain foods can be frozen for.

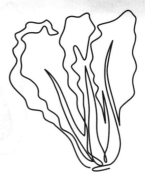

Plan your meals for the week and be aware of the amount of food you are purchasing – it might seem tedious, but planning for the week and only buying what you need for all of your meals will avoid waste.

Batch cook big dishes, such as curries or stew, which can be eaten over a few days, reducing the need to cook every day.

Store food properly – use airtight containers and keep the fridge tidy so you know what you've got and how long the items will last.

Eat before you shop. If you're hungry, you're likely to buy more than you need, and you'll be more inclined to buy sugary snacks.

Do a tally of all the food and drink items that you throw away over a month and make changes based on any patterns that you see.

Remember that some items don't need to be thrown away when they're slightly past their prime.

SUSTAINABLE SHOPPING

Money talks, so every time we spend we are making a choice. Here's how to cast your vote for a more sustainable world every day with your purchases:

Clothes

- Look for items that are made from recycled materials.

- Buy second-hand from charity shops, car boot sales or marketplaces on the internet.

- Buy locally, or from independent shops who will have a smaller carbon footprint than corporations.

- Choose ethical, eco-friendly companies.

- Mend clothes when they break – sew on a new button, patch the hole, fix the zip.

- Choose clothes that you will wear lots rather than ones that you will wear once and discard.

Food

- Choose food with the least packaging.

- Buy fresh food from local producers where possible.

- Eat food that's in season.

- Eat more vegetarian or vegan meals, as animal products generally require more energy to produce than plant products.

- Opt for plant milk rather than dairy milk.

- Go to a refillery for store-cupboard items such as rice, pulses and pasta.

- If you have a garden, grow your own vegetables.

- Bring a reusable bag when you go shopping rather than taking plastic ones from the shop.

Electronics

- Buy your phone and choose a SIM-only deal rather than upgrading your phone regularly.

- Upgrade the software on your computer or laptop rather than buying a new machine.

- Avoid buying fad electronic devices that will be discarded.

SAVE ENERGY

Here are a few tips on how to save energy around the home. These tips will help you to save your money and reduce your carbon footprint too.

Wash clothes at a lower temperature.

Lower the brightness settings on your electronic devices as this will make the charge last longer.

When you're charging phones, tablets and laptops, unplug them once they have reached full battery.

Wash the dishes by hand.

Buy A-rated energy-efficient appliances.

Dry clothes outside or in a well-ventilated room rather than using a tumble dryer.

Try not to open your oven while food is cooking – this lowers the temperature and more energy is used to heat it back up.

Sign up to a green energy tariff.

Use compact fluorescent lamps (CFLs) or light-emitting diodes (LEDs), which use less energy and last longer than traditional bulbs.

Turn the lights off when you leave a room.

Only turn your heating on when you're in the house.

Set your thermostat a couple of degrees lower and wear an extra layer to stay toasty.

When boiling the kettle, only fill it with as much water as you need.

Use draught excluders around windows and doors.

Install thick, lined curtains to help insulate your home.

Fit your windows with double glazing for more effective insulation.

Shower instead of having a bath.

Turn the taps off when you're not using them.

Consider installing solar panels, which will lower your carbon footprint and potentially earn you money.

CUT DOWN ON PLASTIC

Plastic is a serious problem. It's a cheap and versatile product, but it's one of the worst culprits for polluting and contaminating our world. Every year, eight million tonnes of plastic are dumped in the sea, and the amount of plastic that's sent to landfill is sufficient to circle the world four times – and unlike other man-made materials, it doesn't biodegrade. Even the everyday items that we recycle can take years to break down; nylon fabric can take 30–40 years, aluminium cans can take up to 100 years, and plastic bags can take 500 or possibly even never fully biodegrade. To help look out for the planet, here are a few tips to help you reduce your plastic use.

Bathroom

- Instead of liquids choose solid products that require no/little packaging, such as soap, shampoo, conditioner and deodorant bars, toothpaste tabs and bath bombs.

- Avoid products that contain microbeads and microplastics.

- Use more paper-, cotton- and bamboo-based products, such as cotton buds with paper stems, bamboo toothbrushes, and cotton and bamboo pads.

- Swap to reusable sanitary products or 100 per cent cotton tampons or pads.

- Ditch the disposable razors and use metal ones instead.

- Buy coconut oil in bulk and use it to remove make-up, and as a deodorant, moisturizer and conditioner.

- Store away small empty containers to decant toiletries into when you go on holiday.

Cleaning products

- Opt for recycled toilet paper packaged in paper.

- Use carbolic soap for surface cleaner.

- Use white vinegar to clean the toilet.

- Use coconut oil mixed with bicarbonate of soda to remove stains.

- Reuse cleaning cloths, boiling them in water after each use, until they perish.

- Swap sponges for bamboo scrubbers.

- Keep old clothes, towels and bed sheets to use as cloths, and toothbrushes to use for cleaning off grime and mould.

Kitchen items

- Use washing powder and soda crystals that come in cardboard packaging.

- Use beeswax wraps instead of cling film.

- Buy loose fruit and veg.

- Buy bakery items that come in paper bags.

- Buy store-cupboard food in bulk to maximize the food to packaging ratio.

- Buy loose leaf tea or teabags that are biodegradable.

- Stay clear of items packaged in a significant amount of single-use plastic, such as coffee pods and microwave meals.

- Buy long-lasting kitchenware, such as stainless steel for the hob, and clay and stoneware for the oven.

SUSTAINABLE TRAVEL

We all know that to reduce our carbon footprint we should do our best to walk or cycle short distances and take public transport where we can. But what about when we need to fly? There's no getting around the fact that flying dramatically increases our carbon footprint, but we can make choices to help minimize the impact of our journeys and protect the earth. Here are a few ideas:

Make sure you *really* need to fly – if you're travelling for work, could a video call suffice? If it really is an important meeting, see if you can arrange to meet other clients within the vicinity, so as not to double up on trips.

Research which airlines have smaller carbon footprints and fly with them.

Fly from your nearest airport and use public transport to get there to minimize the emissions from driving.

Fly economy class – even if your company is paying for it. The carbon footprint for first class is four times bigger.

Travel light – a heavier plane means more fuel is used.

Fly direct – don't take multiple flights to a country just because it's cheaper. Not only are you travelling further, but you are multiplying your take-offs and landings, which are the parts of the journey that use up the most amount of fuel.

MORE NATURE

Over thousands of years, the natural world has shaped us and defined who we are, and maintaining a connection to it is something that humankind needs not only to survive but to thrive. Modern life dictates that we spend much of our time indoors, hunched over screens and, overwhelmed by light, stress and stimuli, we are losing this connection. But, if we give it the chance, the great outdoors can make our lives richer, more fulfilling and meaningful.

It can be hard to get away from the responsibilities of our day, but however much or little time you have, there will always be a way to get back to nature even if only for a short while. To restore and refresh ourselves, we need to spend less of our day inside, making time to revel in the great outdoors and all it has to offer.

SEEK OUT
green spaces

Being outdoors is a natural antidote for the stress and pressure of the everyday. Not only can it calm the mind and give you an energy boost, but it can also promote a healthy immune system and sharpen our focus. Recent scientific research has also shown that a single exposure to nature – from a countryside walk to pottering in the garden – can promote feelings of positivity for as many as the next seven hours.

Seek out green spaces near you, such as gardens or parks. No matter whether they're big enough to get lost in, or small enough that you can see one side from the other, immersing yourself in greenery and the natural world will help to bring you a sense of peace and calm. Sit beneath a tree in the park and let the blades of grass tickle your palms or even your toes. Feel the fresh air filling your lungs and the natural light on your skin.

Another way to find that sense of well-being is to walk. Take 20 minutes of your lunch break to go for a stroll outside, or make time at the beginning or the end of your day. As you walk, pay attention to your surroundings. Notice the details of the buildings and the people you pass, and listen to the sounds all around you. Attune yourself to your own feelings – how does your environment make you feel?

Forest bathing

A forest is a place of stillness and calm, somewhere the noise and bustle of daily life can't quite reach. It's a peaceful, natural space where you can unwind, refresh and restore yourself.

This idea – that the forest has the power to heal – is at the heart of the Japanese practice of forest bathing, *shinrin-yoku*. The concept is simple: walk through the forest, take your time and absorb the atmosphere around you. The clean, green air. Sunlight. Birdsong. The wind in the trees. The ground under your feet. As you wander, focus only on this and allow your mind to switch off and relax.

There are many health benefits of forest bathing. It can boost your immune system; reduce blood pressure; increase your energy levels; improve your mood, your sleep and your ability to focus; and even accelerate your body's ability to heal. Studies have also shown that, when measured, rates of hostility and aggression diminish among those who have been in a forest environment. Being at one with nature, surrounded by a naturally beautiful ambience, promotes positivity and happiness.

COME TO THE WOODS, FOR HERE IS REST. THERE IS NO REPOSE LIKE THAT OF THE GREEN DEEP WOODS.

John Muir

RUN WILD

Running is more than just a way to exercise – it's an excuse to explore. Instead of running the same route every time, challenge yourself to seek out new ones. Even if you're running in a city, every minute spent outdoors will help to invigorate you.

If you want to delve more deeply into nature, try trail running. This sport is about following a trail through a natural landscape, and it's everything you love about running but with the added bonus of being surrounded by the natural world.

Routes can take you both high and low, and the terrain can be as varied as the weather conditions you'll encounter. You could be running over rocky paths, grass or through streams, in rain, sun, cloud and fog. Every trail is different – even the same trail will be unique every time you run it.

As you run you'll not only feel the exhilaration of movement and the gradual clearing of your mind, but you'll feel excitement and energy as you explore the world around you – inherent in trail running is a sense of adventure.

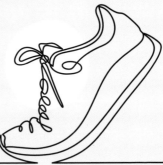

CLOUD SPOTTING

They often go unnoticed, but if you take time to look up, you'll catch one of nature's most impressive and beautiful displays: the clouds. A sunny sky is often what we hope for when we're planning a day in the open, but a cloudy sky is infinitely more interesting. Every cloud is as unique as a snowflake. They are constantly evolving, and the ways they change and catch the light can create moments of striking, majestic beauty.

Clouds make a fantastic display wherever you are. Look for thin, wispy cirrus clouds on high, for altocumulus clouds that sit in woolly rows, or watch for the picture-perfect cumulus clouds, fluffy and bright white. On a stormy day, you might see a cumulonimbus, ominous, thick and billowing its way high into the sky.

GO FORAGING

Historically, humans evolved to be hunter-gatherers and relied on foraging to provide enough food to survive. It's a skill that many of us have no need for today, but foraging is a great way to learn about the natural world and to get back in touch with it. Plus, it's highly rewarding – like a real-life treasure hunt where the prize is a delicious dish that you'll have found and cooked for yourself from scratch.

The golden rules of foraging:

- Only eat your finds if you are absolutely confident that you know what they are.

- To avoid damaging plant populations, forage from as wide an area as possible and don't take more than you need.

- Be cautious when trying new foods, especially if you have medical conditions.

- Ensure that you have permission from the landowner before foraging on private land.

FOODS YOU CAN FORAGE FOR:

Sloes (blackthorn)

Flavour gin and port or make syrup.

Blackberries

Make jam, jelly, vinegar or wine, or add to cakes and muffins.

Crab apple

Flavour whiskey or make jams and jellies.

Dandelion

Sauté for a side dish, stir into egg dishes, or make cordial, tea or wine.

Wild garlic

Use in salads, sauces or pesto, or stir into risotto or omelettes.

Hazelnuts

Roast them, make nut butter, sprinkle over pasta dishes or use in cakes, biscuits and tarts.

Camomile

Make tea, or use the flavour in sauces, cakes and shortbreads.

Sweet chestnuts

Roast them or use in pies, soups or salads.

Elderflower

Make cordial for drinks, cakes and sauces.

Nettles

Make soup, sauté for a side dish, or add to risotto.

Laver seaweed

Use in stir-fries, soups, stews, fried rice, pasta or noodle dishes.

WILD
swimming

Wild swimming is about much more than swimming lengths.
It's about reconnecting with nature and getting the most out
of being in the open. It's a full-body experience of the natural
world that involves all of your senses, and, because the natural
world is unique every day, no two swims are ever the same.

There are many health benefits to swimming, all of which
are enhanced by venturing out into the open air rather than
swimming indoors. Not only does it improve your fitness, but
the cold water invigorates you, and embracing the chill can
even be the source of a natural high. Swimming outdoors
and engaging with nature as you swim has also been shown
to improve your mood and alleviate feelings of depression.

Another benefit is that it's a low-cost activity. The simple,
wholesome pleasure is open to anyone and everyone. If it
becomes something you love, it could take you all over the
world in search of ever more beautiful locations to swim in.

If you choose to venture out into wild waters, remember
to always research the river or lake before you go,
to ensure you are a strong enough swimmer.

Birdwatching

Birdwatching is truly one of life's simple pleasures. It can be anything you want it to be; take your binoculars and field guide and venture out to see what you can find, visit well-known birdwatching spots, or simply keep an eye out for them in your day-to-day life.

Wherever and however you watch them, stories unfold before you as you spend time with birds in their natural habitat. If you're lucky enough to watch them for a long period of time, you may even start to see their personalities shining through. Birdwatching is at its heart an exercise of patience and stillness, and, as such, it lends itself to quiet contemplation. Combined with the benefits of spending time outdoors, surrounded by everything green, windswept and natural, birdwatching is restorative. When you're concentrating on the birds as they dash in and out of a hedge, or circle elegantly overhead, you will find yourself absorbed in the moment.

MORE QUIET

When was the last time you truly experienced complete silence? Most of us probably won't be able to recall.

We contend with all kinds of noise on a daily basis – noise pollution from cities, with cars, roadworks and music, noise from emails and notifications that clamour for our attention, noise from the people we surround ourselves with, noise in the form of mental chatter as we think and worry and wonder and plan... It's no wonder that we are overstressed and overwhelmed.

This chapter suggests that, instead of turning up the volume so we can be heard, we should turn the noise off and embrace the silence, because we can only get back in tune with ourselves by becoming quiet enough to listen.

MUTE
social media

———

A large number of us spend hours every day on social media. For all its gifts, not only is it one of the biggest drains on our time and energy, but it's also a source of intense pressure, whether we realize it or not.

Social media is designed to be addictive. We are compelled to keep checking our phones, to stay connected, to appear popular, good-looking, cool and sociable, and to present the best version of ourselves to the world. But social media can cause self-criticism, loss of focus and concentration and loneliness, and there is mounting evidence that it is linked to anxiety and depression.

Social media itself is not negative, but the way that we use it is often unhealthy, so for a clearer and more peaceful mind, we should take care to regularly spend time away from our phones. By allowing ourselves to be unconnected, we can break old habits and form newer, more mindful ones.

TAKE BACK CONTROL

If you're glued to social media, try the following tips to free yourself from its grasp:

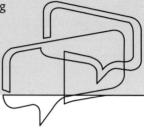

Use a tracking app to log how much time you spend on each social media app. We often underestimate how much time we have spent online and this can be an eye-opener.

Before you go on your phone, ask yourself why and what you want to achieve. If it's just to kill time, leave your phone alone.

Next time you get the urge to check your phone, tell yourself that you have to wait ten minutes. Quite often, you will forget you ever intended to check it in the first place.

Turn off push notifications and alert sounds so that you're not distracted by your phone unnecessarily.

Organize your apps so that social media isn't on your home screen. Out of sight, out of mind.

Set your screen to greyscale – this makes everything look less appealing, and can be a handy deterrent!

Install an app that puts a time limit on your social media apps. If you know that you only have ten minutes per day for Facebook, you will use it more sparingly.

Try deleting the apps that take up the majority of your time. If you have to log in every time, you'll be less likely to use them without thinking.

Be purposeful: decide exactly how you will spend your time before you go on your phone, do it, then set the phone down again and get on with your day.

Dedicate one evening a week to being phone free, or commit to making one area of your house (such as your bedroom) a phone-free zone.

Limit yourself to sharing one thing per day. This forces you to think more carefully about what you share, and it can also be liberating, as it frees you from the pressure to curate your life so intensely.

Try any of these tips with a friend. Knowing that you're not alone and that you can share experiences can improve your resolve and motivation!

The joy of being alone

We tend to shy away from being alone, because it seems
scary, boring, lonely, sad... But it doesn't have to be
any of those things. What's more: it shouldn't be.

Being able to spend time with yourself helps you to be
happy in your own skin and at peace with who you are. It's
a time for contemplation and reflection and for pursuing
the things that you want to do. There is evidence to show
that being alone can boost your creativity and productivity
and make you more compassionate. The ability to spend
some time in your own company is also linked to a life of
increased happiness, satisfaction and lower stress levels.

Next time you have an evening of free time, keep
it free. Allow yourself to be alone, and enjoy the
restorative experience of having *you* all to yourself.

TAKE YOURSELF ON A DATE

Just because you're on your own doesn't mean you have to stay in. Next time you're on your own, take yourself out on a date. You could sit in your favourite coffee shop and read a book, go to the cinema or the theatre, go for a walk in the country or along the beach, visit a local gallery or museum, or go for dinner at a restaurant you've always wanted to try, or simply find a comfortable spot to sit in and watch the world go by. Being alone is no barrier to going out and having fun!

SPEND TIME IN SILENCE

Being silent is a radical act. It goes against every message we receive from the outside world about being connected, busy and ready for anything. It can be daunting at first – it feels foreign and often awkward – but being comfortable with silence is a valuable and calming skill.

It's also a way to look after your body. Noise increases our levels of cortisol, the stress hormone, so by surrounding ourselves constantly with sound and input, we're making ourselves stressed even if we're not aware of it.

In contrast, silence has been proved to release tension from the body – even just two minutes can make a difference. Disengaging from external stimuli also allows us to reconnect with our internal world, and find peace within ourselves. We should embrace silence and its simple, calming power, because, when we lean into it, some of its stillness is imparted to us too.

Silence is a source
of great strength.

Lao Tzu

EVERYDAY SILENCE

Aim for a period of silence every morning or evening – an hour or just ten minutes. Try a silent commute, where you choose the sounds of the world around you, rather than music, conversation or news. If silence is daunting for you, why not try a silent, non-tech-based hobby such as journaling, reading, meditation or yoga?

VALUE BOREDOM

One of the most valuable things you can do for your brain in our always-on world is to allow yourself to be bored. In the quiet moments of the day when we're washing the dishes, walking to work, brushing our teeth – in other words, when we're not bombarding ourselves with stimuli – our brains are able to switch gear.

This gear is known as "default mode", a kind of wakeful resting, and it's the human version of autopilot. In this mode, our mind is able to wander and daydream, and as it wanders it makes connections between past experiences and our present. This means that default mode helps us to come up with solutions to problems, to work through issues and to be creative. This mode also helps us to take stock of our lives and get a bearing on our personal narrative, so it allows us to set goals and aspirations for the future too.

It may feel like you're doing nothing, but when you're "bored" your mind is working hard. When you're next confronted with a tedious, routine task, see it not as a drain on your time or a chore, but as an opportunity to let your mind unwind and shift gear.

IN THE MIDST
OF MOVEMENT
AND CHAOS,
KEEP STILLNESS
INSIDE OF YOU.

Deepak Chopra

MORE JOY

When it comes to happiness, our instinct is often to strive outward. We look for things that we can add to our lives to increase our joy, thinking that the answer lies somewhere beyond ourselves. We buy things we don't need or we search for some kind of magic object or person that will make us feel differently.

However, we are often our own biggest obstacle when it comes to joy. Happiness starts with ourselves, *in* ourselves; the key to finding more of it is having an open mind and an open heart, and reducing negativity so that we can allow joy to flourish.

ATTITUDE OF POSITIVITY

We bring our thoughts and expectations with us everywhere. This means that with any situation or event in our day, we have a choice: we can choose to approach it with a negative attitude or a positive one.

Our thoughts colour our experience of the world. If you're about to try something new and you're thinking, "This is going to go badly", "I will be terrible at this" or "I don't want to be here", then the chances are that you won't have a good time.

Living a happier life often involves curating a more positive mindset, so take notice of your thoughts, and if you notice that they're taking a negative turn, try reframing them. For instance, when you're doing something new, you could say, "I don't know how this will go, but I'll do my best" or "This might be a new opportunity for me."

Even small changes in our language can be effective at shifting our mindset. For instance: phrases that commonly inspire dread, "I have to go to the gym" or "I have to go to work", are transformed when you say, "I get to go to the gym" or "I get to go to work."

THE THINGS YOU THINK ABOUT DETERMINE THE QUALITY OF YOUR MIND. YOUR SOUL TAKES ON THE COLOUR OF YOUR THOUGHTS.

———

Marcus Aurelius

Affirmations
for happiness

———

An affirmation is a short word or phrase that you can say to help to centre and focus yourself. They can be used for all manner of situations: to help you to control anger, to motivate you, to boost your self-confidence or, in this case, to inspire a positive outlook.

When you need a boost, you can write your affirmation down, recite it to yourself or, best of all, say it out loud while looking in the mirror. Look yourself in the eye, hold your head up, release the tension from your shoulders and say your affirmation to your reflection with as much confidence and assurance as you can.

The key to affirmations is focusing on the positive outcome that you want rather than the negative possibility that you wish to avoid. Write your own, specific to your circumstances, or try any of the following phrases to set an intention for your day:

I am calm and
I am happy.

I will have
a good day.

I inhale
positivity and
exhale negativity.

I am brimming
with energy.

I am good enough.

I am right
where I need to be.

I am ready
for the day and
whatever it brings.

SELF-LOVE

If happiness is a flower, then self-love is the soil. The flower can't grow unless it's nourished by the soil – and we can't truly find happiness if we aren't compassionate toward ourselves.

So be kind to yourself, believe in yourself, and know that you, just as you are, are enough. You are worthy of happiness, love and peace – and no matter where life takes you, you always will be. This doesn't mean that you will never grow and change, or that you will never make mistakes. But it does mean that, whatever happens, you're complete just the way you are.

LOVE YOURSELF FIRST AND EVERYTHING ELSE FALLS INTO LINE.

Lucille Ball

FIND JOY IN
the everyday

When we think of joy and happiness, we often think in terms of grand gestures and big events. The pictures that we see in our mind's eye are those where we are radiantly happy, and when we're so full of feeling that we could almost burst.

What we sometimes forget is that joy can be quiet too. There are small pockets of happiness tucked into every day as long as we have eyes to see them: a smile from a passer-by, a kind gesture, a job well done, a delicious meal, a hug from a friend.

Our lives are made up of the small moments stitched together, and it's these, rather than the big gestures, that truly add up to make a happy life.

So, while we go about our days, striving to do our best, it's worth remembering that some of the most life-affirming joy can be found in what we already have in front of us.

There are always flowers for those who want to see them.

HENRI MATISSE

GRATITUDE
JOURNALING

———

Keeping a gratitude journal is a great way to help us focus on the positive aspects of the day, and helps to get us into the habit of finding joy in the little things.

Try keeping a gratitude journal for a week, and see how it influences your outlook. You can make it as simple or as complex as you want – simply write down three things that you were grateful for today, or journal the events in detail. You could keep a physical diary, jot down notes on your phone, or just make a mental note to think of a few points from your day that have made you smile. If you want to get started, why not try the journal opposite?

Monday

....

Tuesday

....

Wednesday

....

Thursday

....

Friday

....

Saturday

....

Sunday

....

Ikigai: a reason for living

Ikigai is a Japanese concept which translates roughly as "a reason for living". It's a core belief or feeling that characterizes who you are and what's most important to you, and many believe that finding and defining your *ikigai* – the thing that gives you purpose – is the key to feeling fulfilled and happy.

Your *ikigai* will be unique to you, because we all find happiness in different ways. You may find it through your work, or through a hobby; your *ikigai* could be providing and caring for your family, or you could find it through creating beauty, by making laughter, or by spreading peace.

Primarily, it should be something that brings you joy and leaves you feeling fulfilled, and it will usually connect you to the people around you. For instance, a writer's work will be read and discussed and a volunteer's time will help another person. Your *ikigai* is also often related to things you can see developing, whether you're working on a project, improving a skill or watching a child growing up.

Finding your
ikigai

Start by asking questions. What moments do you most enjoy in everyday life? What do you do without anyone asking you to do? What were your favourite things to do as a child? What makes you feel emotions strongly? What are you looking forward to? If money was no object, what would you still want to do? The answers to these kinds of questions will give you a feel for what makes you tick; the next step is to look at your answers and see if you can find patterns.

Don't feel you have to search too far beyond the life you already live. You will probably naturally have a sense of what your *ikigai* might be, as you will already know what inspires you. It just takes time to be able to crystallize those feelings into a single sentence. And, while you're taking that time, remember that, even if you don't have your *ikigai* defined completely, every day spent paying attention to what inspires you and brings you joy will help you to live a richer, more fulfilled life.

WHEN NEGATIVITY STRIKES

No matter how hard we try, there will always be days when we don't feel happy, and this is inevitable. Happiness is not constant; it's not a destination that can be reached, or something that can be sustained forever. It's natural for feelings to ebb and flow, and we need darker moments to balance out the lighter ones. However, if you do find yourself in a darker day, there are things you can do to help chase away the clouds.

Break the cycle: If your thoughts are circling round and round, break the cycle. Focus on one positive thing that's happened to you this week, and hold on to this. Then think of another, and then another.

Move: Exercise is a stress reliever, a mood booster and a tonic for the mind and body. If you're not feeling yourself, try a short, hard burst of activity. Go for a sprint, run up and down the stairs, sing a song at the top of your lungs, or go for a walk around the block.

Hydrate: Our negative feelings are exacerbated by being dehydrated, so if you're feeling down, make sure you've had plenty of water.

Phone a friend: Pick up the phone and chat to a friend. You can talk through the things that are bothering you, or you can use your call to take your mind away from your worries. Social connections are good for us, and engaging with friends can help to lift your mood.

HAPPINESS... NOT IN ANOTHER PLACE BUT THIS PLACE, NOT FOR ANOTHER HOUR BUT THIS HOUR.

Walt Whitman

EVERYDAY
adventures

Expand your horizons every day! There are so many ways to bring excitement and adventure to daily life. Here are some ideas:

Go outside and feel the grass underneath your bare feet. Walk a different route to normal, and notice all the details of your surroundings.

Have a lunchtime scavenger hunt. Find something beautiful, something wild, something that smells good and something that's perfectly imperfect.

Try a new recipe, or cook with an ingredient you've never used before.

Jump in puddles.

Take an hour-long summer holiday. Invite a group of friends or colleagues to play summer games, such as Frisbee and treat yourself to an ice cream.

Go to a new café, or try a snack that you've never had before.

Write a letter or a postcard to a friend.

Have a skills swap: exchange marketable skills, hobby skills, or teach each other phrases in a foreign language.

Buy yourself flowers.

Wake up early and have a long, leisurely breakfast.

Wrap up warm and go stargazing.

Listen to an album the whole way through.

Drop in on a friend or relative on the way home from work for a half-hour chat.

On a windy day, fly a kite.

Create a messaging group for a select few friends and set a theme. Try a "name that song" group, or challenge your friends to send a photo of their weirdest find in an antique store.

Invite a friend over for a midweek sleepover.

Attend an evening of local entertainment – find a comedy night, live music at a pub, or a community theatre performance.

MORE YOU

From time to time, we all get lost in the flurry of a busy life, but we can always uncover a path back to our best and happiest selves.

Perhaps you need to take a step back and free yourself of the clutter you don't need. Maybe you need to reduce distractions so that you can focus on what is really important to you. Perhaps you need to break away from negativity and allow yourself the gift of self-kindness and compassion.

Embracing the power of "less" gives us permission to focus on what we need – and when we do this, we allow ourselves room to breathe, to think, and to find joy in a simpler life.

NOTES

IMAGE CREDITS

If you're interested in finding out more about our books, find us on Facebook at Summersdale Publishers and follow us on Twitter at @Summersdale.

www.summersdale.com